Laudable Pursuit:
A 21st Century Response to Dwight Smith

by
The Knights of the North

Laudable Pursuit: A 21st Century Response to Dwight Smith

Copyright © 2005-2006 by the Knights Of The North

"*Make no little plans. They have no magic to stir men's blood and probably themselves will not be realized. Make big plans; aim high in hope and work, remembering that a noble, logical diagram once recorded will never die, but long after we are gone will be a living thing, asserting itself with ever-growing insistency. Remember that our sons and grandsons are going to do things that would stagger us. Let your watchword be order and your beacon beauty. Think big. "*

--Daniel Burnham, Chicago architect (1864-1912);
Director of Works for the Chicago Columbian Exposition of 1893;
Architect of the Chicago Masonic Temple, which was, in 1891,
at 22 stories, the tallest skyscraper in the world.

PART ONE

WHAT COME YOU HERE TO DO?

Over the last decade, Grand Lodges all over North America have tried to turn the tide of shrinking membership with one-day classes, reduced proficiency requirements, open solicitation, "cut-rate deals" on multiple degrees, radio, TV and billboard advertising blitzes, and many other schemes. The doors to the Temple have been flung wide open, yet the numbers have continued to decline.

The state of the Masonic corpus is lethargic, verging on catatonia, for a lot of reasons, not the least of which is a sloth born of six decades of euchre nights, pancake breakfasts, fish frys and bean suppers. Gone are the traveling Masonic orators and globe-trotting lecturers who used to pack our lodges and auditoriums—we can see or hear more exciting stuff on 275 digital channels these days. Gone are the days when Scottish Rite auditoriums were jammed with a thousand petitioners, when the Rite offered theatrical productions with spectacle and the finest in state-of-the-art special effects.

Younger men who have studied about the Craft before joining it are not finding the Lodges of Washington and Franklin and Revere, of Goethe and Mozart and the Royal Society members. True, it is folly to pine for some long-ago "golden age" of Freemasonry, because every age had its own challenges and shortcomings. And there is plenty of room for argument as to which little snapshot of Masonic history to which each of us would like to return.

One thing remains certain: Freemasonry is shrinking. The huge numbers in the 40's and 50's and 60's are gone forever, a statistical aberration that will never happen again. Moreover, the majority of men who have spent decades sending in money to carry cards in their wallets for the York Rite, the Scottish Rite, the Shrine, the Grotto and the OES aren't going to those places any more than they are attending their Blue Lodges. Masonry will not be saved by the appendant bodies or their charities. The tail cannot wag the dog—Freemasonry must save itself. It is now our job as the next generation of leaders to decide where Freemasonry is headed and how to get it there. Because the Baby Boomers rejected Masonry and most things of their fathers, we are jumping a generation and maybe two - and that provides an opportunity.

We are poised on a ledge, and can either fall into oblivion, or turn around and head a direction different from the one we are going. Not to become just another service club, like Lions or Kiwanis. Not to become more like the "animal" fraternities by turning our Lodges into bars and billiard halls. Not to become crass, noisy, self-aggrandizing back-patters for our charities.

We have a brief window of opportunity to return this fraternity to what it once was: the best, the most respected, the most universal and most legendary fraternity in the world. This new generation of members wants to associate with something ancient, something mythical, something legendary; with a group that has been the fraternity of the greatest of men for three centuries; with a fraternity that is worldwide in its scope, and universal in its welcoming of all faiths and all races; with a local lodge that helps the family next door and the school down the street; with a group that once was at the forefront of issues that shaped this country and, arguably, was the crucible that gave birth to the American Revolution, because they were men of action and social conscience; with a fraternity that claims as its members the most imaginative minds and the most successful of men.

That's what they read about on the Internet and in books and see in movies and even comics. That's the image they see, and what they are looking for when they knock on our doors.

But what do we give them when they enter? Stop for a minute and think about the image your Lodge projects. Think about what they expect versus what they find. Given that disparity, how long do we suspect they will stay? Current statistics from all over the U.S. are answering that question: not very long. Freemasonry is losing more men today to demits and non-payment of dues than to the death rate. In short, we are boring our members to death.

This document is an attempt to turn the tiller of the Craft in another direction – or, rather, to put it back on course. It is a call to stop worshiping at the altar of Change for the sake of Change, while taking a studied approach to improving the overall health of Freemasonry.

In the early 1960's, Dwight Smith, Past Grand Master and, at that time, Grand Secretary, of the Grand Lodge of Indiana, wrote a series of articles for the Indiana Freemason Magazine, that eventually were collected in two classic booklets, *Whither Are We Traveling?* and *Why This Confusion In The Temple?* His questions and observations are as valid today as they were when he wrote them, perhaps more so, given the current atmosphere within Freemasonry concerning declining membership numbers.

Smith's universal answer to the problems of Freemasonry as an institution was to "Try Freemasonry." That is, return the fraternity to its most basic tenets, strip it of its innovations, and get back to the business of concentrating on making men better ones, one Mason at a time.

A few decades after Smith, Nelson King, former president of the Philalethes Society, editor of that organization's magazine, and a respected Masonic scholar, announced that after years of having a liberal view of change within the Craft, he had become a "Born Again Fundamentalist Freemason," or B.A.F.F. He defined it as having a conservative, traditional view as set down by Dwight Smith. Since King's coining of the term B.A.F.F., a movement has started to grow within Freemasonry, suggesting that such an approach may be the answer to the perceived ills that face us on a national and international level.

Smith's Ten Questions as presented in *Whither Are We Traveling?* and his subsequent Ten Pitfalls as presented in *Why This Confusion in the Temple?* are the basic foundation of the modern Born Again Fundamentalist Freemason movement.

Smith's Ten Questions

1. "Can we expect Freemasonry to retain its past glory and prestige unless the level of leadership is raised above its present position?"

2. "How well are we guarding the West Gate?"

3. "Has Freemasonry become too easy to obtain?"

4. "Are we not worshipping at the altar of bigness?"

5. "What can we expect when we have permitted Freemasonry to become subdivided into a score of organizations?"

6. "Has the American passion for bigness and efficiency dulled the spirit of Masonic charity?"

7. "Do we pay enough attention to the Festive Board?"

8. "What has become of that 'course of moral instruction, veiled in allegory and illustrated by symbols,' that Freemasonry is supposed to be?"

9. "Hasn't the so-called 'Century of the Common Man' contributed to making our Fraternity a little too common?"

10. "Are there not too many well-meaning Brethren who are working overtime to make Freemasonry something other than Freemasonry?"

Smith's Ten Pitfalls

1. "Abandon the 'free will and accord' rule which has placed our Craft far above the mine run of societies and permit outright solicitation."

2. "Ape the service clubs. Get busy on 'projects' galore in the best Babbitt fashion."

3. "Go into the organized do-good business in a big way. Find an area of the human body that has not been exploited. Exploit it. Set a quota, have a kickoff dinner, ring the doorbells."

4. "Subsidize other organizations right and left, and, in the doing, ignore, neglect and starve the parent body."

5. "Feminize the Fraternity. Carry 'togetherness' to even more ridiculous extremes than we have already."

6. "Hire press agents to tell the world, like Little Jack Horner, what great boys we are. ('Masonry is not getting its proper share of publicity', complains one Grand Master.) Never mind actions; concentrate on words."

7. "Imitate Hollywood. Stage an extravaganza. Bring in all the groups that ever fancied themselves remotely related to Freemasonry. Form the parade, blow the bugle, beat the drums, and cheapen the Fraternity."

8. "Let Freemasonry 'take a position' on public issues of the day. Stand up and be counted (assuming, of course, that the position our Craft takes is in line with our own pet prejudices)."

9. "Go all out for materialism. Raise money; spend it. Build temples, institutions. Subsidize; endow. Whatever can he had by writing a check, get it."

10. "Centralize, centralize, centralize. Pattern Freemasonry after Washington bureaucracy. Let nothing be done modestly by an individual or a Lodge; do everything on state or national level the super-duper way. Make a great to-do about local self government, but accept no local self-responsibility."

It has been almost forty years since Smith presented these ideas to the fraternity, where they were promptly ignored by members and leaders alike, at both the Grand Lodge and local lodge levels. By failing to answer his questions, we have fallen prey to the very pitfalls he predicted.

The *Laudable Pursuit*, then, is the pursuit of the ancient mythic Freemasonry that we speak of in our literature and do not provide. It seeks fellowship, esoteric study and true Masonic universality. To discuss both changes we need to make in Freemasonry as well as changes we DON'T need to make, we first need to understand where we came from and the alterations made along the way. Then, we will propose solutions to Smith's questions, while endeavoring to avoid his pitfalls.

We now have some hard choices to make, and a limited time in which to make them. While our history of dealing with hard choices in this fraternity is a depressing signpost for the future, there is another way than the one we have been following for decades. It will be the Lodges and Masonic bodies that adapt and carry a vision forward that will survive. For too long we as leaders and protectors of this noble institution have fled the battlefield.

Today is the day we turn and fight.

PART TWO

THE PLACE FROM WHENCE WE CAME

TO CALL THEM ON AGAIN IN DUE SEASON

The history of operative Freemasonry since the formation of the Grand Lodge of England in 1717 has seen many changes. We began in taverns and pubs, and our meetings and degrees were celebrated with the Festive Board, with toasts and food and a camaraderie not found in any other society of its day. Freemasonry was a unique creation, unlike any other institution in what was a rigidly proscribed social class system. Nobleman and commoner, landowner and shopkeeper, general and foot soldier, could meet upon the level in this place—something they could not acceptably do on a city street. Political and religious differences that had torn nations and continents apart were left outside the door. Men from every class and religion in what quickly became every corner of the globe shared in common their degree experience in the Lodge, and a charge to strive for nobler deeds, higher thoughts and greater achievements.

What became today's Middle Chamber lecture in the Fellow Craft degree was an attempt by our forefathers to take good men and make them better. It was an admonition for a Mason to study the liberal arts, to take note of the orders of architecture, to scientifically observe the world around him. This was at a time when public education did not exist, when universities were places where only the children of the very rich could be found, and the notion of questioning religious explanations of natural phenomena could still result in heretical punishments in certain quarters of the globe.

The degrees of Masonry were conferred in many ways in the early days. A man could be initiated, passed and raised in one night, or it could take up to a year between degrees. Multiple candidates were not uncommon for degrees, and early French and Belgian paintings depict several candidates receiving their Master Mason degrees at the same time. Entered Apprentices were welcomed into meetings with open arms, and all lodge business was conducted on the EA degree.

The design of the earliest lodges was such that membership seldom grew beyond forty members or so. It was the intent that a Mother lodge would give birth to daughter lodges when the membership rolls became too large. Lodges met in tents, homes, taverns, hotels and finally dedicated buildings constructed specially as temples for the Craft. Many lodges would meet in the same buildings. The object was for Freemasonry to grow by making new lodges of small size, and the reasons were simple. Twenty, thirty or even forty men could know, love and care for one another. The design was for smaller lodges to have a caring and connected membership. A lodge of a hundred members was unheard of, and a thousand was unthinkable.

Lodges had very different personalities—not simply country or city lodges. Masons of like professions formed affinity lodges. Military lodges were quite common, and were instrumental in spreading Freemasonry around the world in an astonishingly brief period of time, while Europe embarked on two centuries of trade, war and colonial expansion.

To join a lodge meant that a man had come well recommended by Masons who really knew him to be a good, honest man; that he had been investigated thoroughly; that he would be a credit to his Lodge, or that there was at least a spark of potential that would grow within him by associating with men of good character.

Lodge was expensive, so much so that dues (or "subscriptions") would have to be paid at each meeting. In return, the Mason was treated to, not a dinner, but a feast, with plentiful wine or ale for the seven ritual toasts that accompanied the Festive Board. And it was just that: festive, lasting well into the night. Many lodges met on the night of the full moon, to assist the brethren in finding their way home on foot or horseback in the dark.

In less than one hundred years after the birth of the first Grand Lodge, virtually every man, woman and child in the Western world knew who Freemasons were and what the Order stood for. Masons were the elite of society—not in the blue-blooded, landed gentry sense of the word, but elite as in the leaders of their towns, the men of integrity, responsibility and trust, whether they were presidents, doctors, coopers or smiths.

This was the state of Freemasonry during the period of its greatest expansion. Small and exclusive lodges, hard to join, expensive to belong to, encouraging personal and intellectual growth, wrapped in the mantle of charity and robust conviviality for all of its members of every degree.

THAT WHICH WAS LOST

The wave of anti-Masonry that erupted in the United States and Europe in the early 1800s happened for different reasons, with different results. In Europe, it was strongly alleged that Masons had fomented first the English revolution that deposed Charles I, then the French revolutions that turned the entire continent upside down with fear. Freemasonry went underground, resulting in feelings that it was a secret society, but lodges remained little changed.

In America, lodges died off, membership diminished, and society turned against Freemasonry after the Morgan affair in 1826. Fueled by the sudden popularity and noisy promotion of the Anti-Masonic Party, Lodges closed by the hundreds, Grand Lodges went dormant, and the fraternity faced extinction. In 1843, the Baltimore Convention assembled Grand Lodge representatives from all around the country to bring uniformity to ritual and develop new rules for governing lodges, and hopefully, *"to recommend such measures as shall tend to the elevation of the Order to its due degree of respect throughout the world at large."* These were the beginnings of the dramatic changes for Masonry in the United States. Recommendations to standardize the ritual were passed by the delegates, keeping our ritual closer to that illuminated by Preston in 1788 than those our European brothers ultimately ended up with.

Because of the fear that "cowans and eavesdroppers" might join the fraternity, be initiated, view a meeting or two, then expose Masonic secrets, it was decided to bar Entered Apprentices and Fellow Craft from participating in lodge business meetings. The results of this change altered much of what followed in the history of US Masonry. By expelling the EAs and FCs from participating in regular meetings of the lodge, the slow, thoughtful advancement through the degrees was abandoned. Time between degrees was uniformly reduced, from months or a year down to a week or less. Masonic study was replaced by the rote memorization of the Q&A lectures, or catechisms. The practice of meeting in taverns and pubs ended, in favor of the construction of individual lodge halls or temples. And to afford those new buildings required more members.

Masonry again began to spread throughout the country because of war. The Civil War introduced soldiers on both sides to the Craft, and membership again began to grow. American Grand Lodges also became allied with the growing prohibitionist movements, and one by one, most Grand Lodges outlawed the serving of alcohol in lodge buildings or at lodge functions, effectively removing the last vestiges of its tavern hall origins.

After the Civil War, Freemasonry caught the wave of fraternalism that swept the country, and as the granddaddy of them all, Masonry became once again the preeminent fraternal order in a sea of Moose, Elks, Eagles, Redmen, Woodmen and many others. By the turn of the 20th century, a contemporary author noted:

> *"The probable extent of the influence of secret society life may be inferred from the fact that more than 6,000,000 Americans are members of 300 such organizations, which confer about 1,000 degrees on the 200,000 novitiates annually, aided, in instances, by a wealth of paraphernalia and dramatic ceremonials which rival modern stage effects."*
>
> -- Albert E. Stevens
> Cyclopaedia of Fraternities (1907)

During and after both World Wars, an explosion of interest in the Freemasons swelled lodges to unheard of levels. Size of membership and magnificence of temples became

9

the forces that fueled the construction of expensive buildings in every major city. Competition from other groups spurred grander facilities. Pressured by members joining multiple clubs, rites, shrines, grottos and other groups, lodge dues became artificially low to attract and keep new Masons. As long as membership ranks grew, the stagnant dues structure would not be a burden to the Lodges.

Masonry and its appendant bodies began a century-long expansion of "institutionalized" charitable good works, virtually allowing the charities themselves to define their mission. Instead of the brother-to-brother or community charities practiced by the early lodges, charities became officially sponsored, and very big business. Masonic homes, medical and research programs, the Shrine Hospitals and others would grow into multi-million dollar businesses that would require an ever-expanding amount of capital to support. Again, this was not a burden as long as more and more new Masons joined every year.

While these programs were laudable and beneficial to society—along with being very high profile advertising for the Craft—it became a simple matter of writing a check to the charity or deducting donations out of dues money, instead of encouraging Masons to actually reflect upon the tenets of the institution. Relief and charity became something that was done automatically by the organization, not from the heart of the Mason.

AND MAY PERHAPS MEET WITH DEATH

The social upheavals of the Vietnam era brought a grinding halt to fraternalism in America. The vast majority of young men of the 1960s and 70s would grow up to reject the institutions venerated by their fathers and grandfathers, and the number of candidates knocking on Freemasonry's doors slowed to a trickle. Massive lodges with 700 and 800 members would dwindle or close in less than two decades. The appendant bodies that relied on the Lodges for new members would find themselves in even worse shape. Scottish Rite and Shrine auditoriums designed for a thousand candidates would have only a handful at their convocations. The Shrine removed the requirement of York or Scottish Rite membership as a prerequisite for joining, and flirted with dropping their association with Masonry altogether.

Lodges became dominated by ritualists, the Old Guard of members who remembered the boom years, who were resistant to change. Dues overall remained at unconscionably low levels, often driven by a desire not to alienate the swelling ranks of retired members. Actuarial tables march inexorably forward, and as time passed, the lodges were overwhelmingly populated by ever-aging members, further contributing to the appearance that Masonic lodges were places no man under thirty would ever consider. Lodges closed or merged. Buildings were sold.

More damaging was the loss of prestige and knowledge of the Craft in the public consciousness. Less than a hundred years after the formation of the Grand Lodge in England, the whole of the civilized world knew who and what Freemasons were and what they stood for. Yet, sixty years after WWII, fewer and fewer people in society knew what a Freemason was, or that the fraternity still existed.

Freemasonry today stands in the unenviable position of being forgotten by almost three generations of men. Unlike our European brethren who constantly battle with anti-Masons, society in the United States has not turned against us or held us responsible for world domination. We have simply been ignored and cast on the heap with Edsels, 8-Track tapes, and buggy whips.

Lodges, at last coming to grips with the severity of the decline, have pleaded with Grand Lodges for help. In response, they have been granted the right to solicit new members, raise multiple candidates, advertise, hold one-day classes, reduce proficiency, and more. But the simple fact is that the groundswell of members who joined around WWII in record numbers was a statistical aberration, unlikely to be repeated. The truth is that as a ratio to the US population, almost the same *percentage*s of the population are Freemasons today as in the years immediately after the Civil War.

A tide is turning, and more and more young men are rediscovering Freemasonry. They first learn of it through unlikely sources - History Channel exposés, sensational (and largely fictitious) popular books such as Dan Brown's *Da Vinci Code* and *Solomon Key*, films like *National Treasure*, or unflattering ones like *From Hell*, or *League of Extraordinary Gentlemen*. Even ridiculous references like the Simpson's *Stonecutters* have made young minds curious. But instead of finding a relative or neighbor who might be a Mason, they are turning to the Internet for their information. It is increasingly common for their first knock on our doors to be an electronic one.

If the numbers hold constant, there appears to be a growing interest once again in Freemasonry. So the question that faces us now is, what will these new men find when they enter our Lodges? We were once the premiere gentlemen's fraternity in the world. But after decades of throwing the doors open to anyone and everyone, diminishing our standards, and allowing our Temples to crumble both literally and figuratively, what can we do to stop the downward spiral of mediocrity we seem to have embraced out of desperation?

And so, we return to the questions set forth by Dwight Smith, because the problems he identified in 1964 bore fruit. We are now suffering a crisis in the fraternity precisely because no one heard Smith's wakeup call and presented solutions to the problems he cited.

What follows are proposals to listen at last, to learn from past missteps, and most important of all, act.

Laudable Pursuit

PART THREE

TO BE REINVESTED OF WHAT WE WERE DIVESTED

1. Level of Leadership

"Can we expect Freemasonry to retain its past glory and prestige unless the level of leadership is raised above its present position?"

"Everything rises or falls on leadership." The progressive officer's line does not always have to progress. Placing a man in the Master's chair with no other qualification than sitting through a Past Master's degree is fundamentally flawed. A Master cannot just be arbitrarily chosen. He must be considered primarily on his personal character. Then he must be considered because of his personal abilities pertaining to leadership.

He should have vision. If he has none, get him some. Masters should develop goals with his Wardens—long-term goals, not just short-term events and fixes to be attempted in one short year, only to be discarded the next.

A Master must know his field. He must know his ritual (or at least a sweeping command of it, if not letter perfect). He must be committed to knowing his Masonic law. He must know the underlying philosophy of Freemasonry, why it came into existence and why it needs to exist in that form today.

Grand Lodges should require a basic learning course that teaches Wardens how to govern a Lodge. Ask study questions about the ritual, law and philosophy of Masonry. Hold classes around the state twice a year and require attendance at two years' classes and passage of the tests as a qualification of installation as Master. Teach our future leaders the basics about running a Lodge, and not just a modified management course that doesn't deal with ritual, history, and how to lead a volunteer group of men.

Most important of all, teach them the proper and effective use of the gavel. Masters and Wardens need to get the message that Past Masters do not control their Lodges, and act accordingly. The role of the Master is to lead, not to be questioned on every plan or action. Masters also need to understand that the East is not the position for a despot. Effective use of committees needs to be stressed, even if it is a committee of just one man.

At the Grand Lodge level, encourage strategic planning of Grand Lodge programs over five, ten and fifteen years. Put a stop to the endless parade of annual designs that change with each new Grand Master. They waste time, money and the efforts of great and good men who donate endless hours to the Craft by reinventing the wheel year after year. We have a multi-million dollar corporation that is being run with an iron whim from one year to the next.

Freemasonry is not a religion, a business or a service club, but a unique creation. And how does a man get to be the head of that organization? In most jurisdictions, his friend at the top appoints him to an advancing line. It is not based on a man's knowledge or qualifications, but on whom he knows or whom he owes. A Grand Lodge election needs to be an *election*. We should allow three or four men to be nominated for the position of Grand Master, or at least the advancing position, let them present their plans, and elect them on the basis of their qualifications. This is already done in several states.

James I of England once purported, it is *"sedition in subjects, to dispute what a king may do in the height of his power."* We give to our Grand Masters the Divine Right of Kings and pray they use such powers wisely. Sadly, our law does NOT take into account the man who believes in his own divinity. NOR does it account for the simple man who gets his feelings hurt and retaliates against those who disagree with his actions. We charge our Fellow Crafts to judge with candor, admonish with friendship, and reprehend with justice. Grand Masters should be held to the same standard.

Specifically, the power of a Grand Master to suspend a Mason without trial should be eliminated. There should be checks and balances in the form of a required seating of a Trial Committee, made up of Past Masters, NOT Past Grand Masters or Grand Lodge officers. The Trial Committee should convene and rule on suspensions in a timely manner – weeks, not months, and not just once a year when Grand Lodge meets. Masonic justice should be transparent, not secret.

2. Asleep at the West Gate
"How well are we guarding the West Gate?"

Conduct serious investigations. Investigations should take longer, and they should be more thorough. Provide stronger guidelines to Lodges for meeting with potential candidates. Meet him more than once, and at least one time, meet him in his home. We should require a more complete statement from petitioners as to what they expect from membership in a Masonic Lodge. And perhaps the petitioner should appear before the Lodge at refreshment prior to his election. Some jurisdictions outside of the U.S. even blindfold the potential candidate and bring him into the lodge, where unseen members can question him.

Consider the merits of a program started in Kansas in 2003 by Grand Master Robert M. Tomlinson, called "Permissive Edict." He states, *"This gives the lodges the ability to allow petitions for the Mysteries to be received and balloted upon in the usual manner (including an investigation) without the man knowing and if elected, the recommending brother informs him that he has been selected for membership in the world's oldest, largest and most widely respected fraternal organization in the world."* This is essentially the way our brethren selected new members in the earliest days of speculative Freemasonry. Several Grand Lodges are experimenting with this program.

It is vital that we increase the length of time our members remain EAs and FCs. New members should have the time to learn the lessons of Freemasonry, and it is therefore necessary that we allow lodges to open on EA degree, as it is done all over the Masonic world outside of the United States.

3. Pearl of Great Price?
"Has Freemasonry become too easy to obtain?"

"In 1897, the North American Review estimated that the average lodge member spent fifty dollars annually on dues and insurance, and two hundred dollars on initiation fees, ritualistic paraphernalia, banquets and travel; this at a time when the average factory worker earned just four hundred to five hundred dollars a year. "

. -- Mark C. Carnes,
. Secret Ritual and Manhood in Victorian America
(Yale University Press, 1989).

In 2005, $50 dues would be equal to $1107. And that $200 initiation, paraphernalia, banquet and travel budget would cost $4431 today. On an adjusted salary of $8800–$11,000 a year.

Today's Freemasonry is simply too easy to join and too cheap to belong to. Price Pritchett in his book *Firing Up Commitment For Organizational Change* writes about belonging to groups within a corporation and assembling a top-notch management team, but the excerpt below describes the way Freemasonry needs to again regard itself:

The harder we have to struggle for something, the more precious it becomes. Somehow, in sacrificing, we prove to ourselves that what we're seeking is valuable. This holds true when we're pursuing membership.

Sacrifice locks commitment. As people strive to make it through rigorous selection standards, and work to prove their worthiness, they persuade themselves that being a part of the group matters.

Initiation rites - like high walls and narrow gates of entry - build commitment to the group through making acceptance hard to come by. Being allowed to join becomes something special. An achievement. A privilege. And it creates a sense of exclusiveness.

Belonging doesn't count much if almost anybody can drift in or drift out of your group at will. If it's easy to join up, then leave and return, only to leave again, commitment can be hard to find.

Initiation rites also create a common bond of experience that unites all who make it through the ordeal. A strong sense of "we-ness" comes from having gone through a common struggle. This identification with the group feeds commitment.

Finally, stiff criteria for admission cause the weak-hearted to de-select themselves. They opt out after weighing the costs. For them, the rights of membership aren't worth going through the rites of Initiation. The benefit? People with low commitment never get inside.

The greater the personal investment in getting accepted, the more one builds a stake in the organization. This means you should make membership a big deal. Let people pay a price to join. That guarantees commitment at the outset, and also makes it easier to build commitment later on.

Make membership hard to come by, and commitment comes naturally.

-- Price Pritchett
Firing Up Commitment For Organizational Change
(Pritchett & Hull Associates, 1994)

To "fix" shrinking numbers, Grand Lodges have tried one-day classes, reduced proficiency, relaxed standards, casual meetings, radio, TV and billboard advertising, bumper sticker slogans, and cut-rate pricing plans. And the numbers continue to drop. Younger men ARE joining, but instead of a course of moral instruction veiled in allegory, they are finding euchre nights, pancake breakfasts, fish frys and bean suppers. They are finding a desperate group of aging members who are thrilled to have someone show up regularly, but resistant to any change that departs from decades of habit. They are finding bickering and endless meetings about bill paying, bad food, and who is going to iron the degree uniforms. They are finding crumbling temples built for a thousand members that sit empty 29 days out of the month. We joke that society thinks we are going to secretly rule the world, just as soon as we decide on the question of tungsten or florescent lights in the dining room, but it is no joke.

We have tried to appeal to younger men by changing things that simply don't matter to them, and we haven't bothered to ask them about if our suppositions are true. We have said they don't have time to join in the traditional manner. The Grand Master of Pennsylvania quipped to the Associated press in 2004, *"The old-fashioned way of becoming a Mason just doesn't fit modern man."* Of course it does, if the experience we give them is meaningful, poignant and impressive. Rites of initiation should be a special achievement, not instant gratification. If it is easy to join, it is easy to leave. Men with low commitment should never have been initiated in the first place.

We have said proficiency requirements are too hard. Yet they weren't too hard for generations prior to now. And if a man is a stranger to the fraternity, he doesn't know what that proficiency is, so how can that be the thing that is keeping him away?

We have said that the fraternity needs to be de-mystified and open. *"The only secrets we have are a few secret words and handshakes."* Yet the young men knocking our doors are finding out about Freemasonry on the Internet, in movies, in books. The Freemasonry they find in our lodges has almost nothing to do with the historical, mythical or legendary Society they read about—and that disappoints them. By removing the mystery and the majesty from our ceremonies and our Craft, we make them that most terrible of things: we make them Ordinary.

Freemasonry used to be special, exclusive, and membership denoted a *specialness* it lacks today. Masons were looked up to as pillars in their communities, regardless of their profession, age, rank or financial worth. We have been reduced to begging for members because we have become too cheap and because we lowered our standards to let in everyone without any sacrifice on their part. Work, sacrifice, struggle and price make membership more valuable. And the more valuable it is, the less likely a man will simply pay dues and not participate.

To again look outside of the U.S., it is very difficult to join a Lodge elsewhere. In England, candidates are told it could take up to a year to be investigated. In France, a man's application and photo are posted where all members can see it, and any Mason with knowledge of that man may file a report. In both countries, Masonry is expensive. It can cost one month's average wages to petition a lodge, and dues (or subscriptions, as they are known in England) are often paid monthly.

4. The Closed Corporation
"Are we not worshipping at the altar of bigness?"

We don't have too many Lodges, we have too many buildings. Masonry needs more, smaller lodges, with a de-emphasis on membership numbers. Smaller lodges have better interaction with their members. Smaller lodges can appeal to narrower groups within the body of the Craft, satisfy different avenues of interest, and will have very different personalities. Affinity lodges can develop bonds for members with the same hobbies, professions or Masonic interests.

More lodges meeting in our existing buildings are a better utilization of our facilities. A Masonic building that sits empty for 29 days out of the month is a burden on its owners, and appears abandoned to the community. In contrast, a Masonic building with activities on different nights of the week all month long appears to be a vital part of the community. More lodges also means sharing the costs of ownership and maintenance.

We have proclaimed that young men are price conscious, so dues must be kept low. Yet the vast majority of new men joining remark that they thought becoming a Freemason should be MUCH more expensive. Raise the dues and fees appropriately. Men aren't going to pay a high price for the privilege of being Freemasons and then not take advantage of it, but this takes out the window shoppers. Only the committed are going to take us up on this offer. But remember, *men are only going to be committed if they get something for their membership dollars.* In return, they deserve impressive ritual ceremonies, clean and well-appointed facilities, excellent food, inspiring education, and true fraternalism.

Make it simpler than it currently is to open new lodges and encourage the creation of affinity lodges. Masons need to have more in common with each other than the dues card in their back pockets. Lodges made up of doctors or police officers or cigar smokers for example, at least in the beginning, will have a built-in camaraderie that might not otherwise exist, and will help jump-start a new lodge's membership. New lodges should be encouraged to use existing buildings and other inventive locations that can be tyled.

Permit and encourage the study of alternative rituals and ritual associations. This creates diversity and interest in both the esoteric origins of the Craft, as well as a better understanding of Freemasonry as it exists in the rest of the world. So do Masonic book clubs and study groups.

As to the role of Grand Lodge, its primary purpose should be as encouragers and promoters of the art. Not of hasty schemes to get more warm bodies into Masonry for mercenary motives, but of THE ART. As Grand Lodge, we need to be redefining what Masonry is for this century just as the Girl Scouts redefined Girl Scouting—it ain't just hawking overpriced cookies anymore. Likewise, we can't be just ritualists and cod batterers anymore. Grand Lodge needs to be about the basics of serving the fraternity, and to serve as the overarching administrative body. It needs to have a grand, long-term vision for Freemasonry.

Provide for the restoration and improvement of our magnificent buildings. They are symbols of our heritage, and it is a criminal waste of these treasures of the Craft to let them rot from disuse. Many could easily be home to ten times the number of Lodges and appendant bodies they host today. Restore the auditoriums, refurbish the banquet facilities. Make them a source of rental income from local organizations, and a source of pride for the Craft. Rent unused ballrooms out for high school proms and wedding receptions. Encourage the opening of new, smaller lodges within the buildings. Encourage greater use of their lodge rooms, common rooms and kitchen facilities. Divide one cavernous lodge room into four intimate ones, with seats for no more than thirty members each.

Would it not be wonderful to be able to go a central Temple, perhaps work out in a basement exercise and weight room, shower, then head upstairs for a dinner served every night? Go to Lodge, then play a little pool or a video game tournament? Computers in the lounges and a wireless network for the younger members to teach older members how to use the Internet or send e-mail to their grandkids? A cigar lounge with a walk-in humidor? Maybe a movie or sports event on a huge projection TV screen? Encourage tenant lodges to compete with each other in redecorating their rooms and instill a sense of ownership instead of the renter/landlord attitude that often exists. Perhaps even take one giant two-storey room and divide it into four, small, intimate ones to better suit the size lodges we have today? In short, encourage unconventional thinking regarding the use of these buildings, and streamline and reduce the hurdles that prevent any change from happening.

Or sell them. A crumbling eyesore is a black eye to the Craft, and an embarrassment within the community.

5. Subdivided We Stand
"What can we expect when we have permitted Freemasonry to become subdivided into a score of organizations?"

For too many years, Ancient Craft Masonry has allowed itself to simply be the front door for the appendant organizations. *"All the way in one day"* classes have been designed to whisk a new member through the degrees so he can really join another group or two, reducing the three lodge degrees to a mere inconvenience to be suffered through. New Masons should take their time and learn the lessons of the Lodge before being pressured to join another group that will further divide his precious free time.

The greatest mistake we make is to tell our new Entered Apprentices that their presence at our meetings is not required. New members should be encouraged, to attend Lodge regularly, and Lodges should strive to have activities every single week. New members should get in the habit of thinking of one night a week as Lodge night, and not just once a month for a boring business meeting. Mentors need to remain in contact with a new member and take on the job of contacting the new brother when he does not attend. It bears pointing out that European lodges fine or suspend members who repeatedly fail to come to lodge. By constant and regular attendance, Masons bond together, learn to love and care for each other. We have lost that personal bond by ignoring new and old members, letting them disappear, then striking them from our lists when they are finally lost or disinterested.

Other Masonic bodies have much to offer, and the Symbolic Lodge is not the only valid Masonic experience. But Lodges should discourage brothers from joining the Rites, Shrine, Grotto, OES or other such bodies until at least one calendar year after their raising. The Grand Lodge should also discourage this, if not by rule than at least by suggestion. The Masonic Lodge is the Foundation Stone of this fraternity, not merely a tollbooth to the other bodies. It should be treated as such. If the Shrine or the Rites are more interesting or fun for members, *shame on us at the local Lodge level for allowing that to happen.* That is not the fault of the other bodies, it is ours, and it needed to be addressed yesterday. Once a man is a Freemason, the concordant bodies have a lifetime to seek his membership. But let's make men into Freemasons first.

6. Sounding Brass and Tinkling Cymbal?
"Has the American passion for bigness and efficiency dulled the spirit of Masonic charity?"

Big, institutionalized Masonic charity was more of a pressing concern in the days before the New Deal and the Great Society social service programs. When the Masonic retirement homes were created, there was no social safety net for wives, widows and orphans. And certainly no AARP. Now there is, and much of what Freemasonry was once very good at has been made redundant.

Lodge members rarely think about real charity anymore, because theirs, often the state's Masonic Home, is taken out of their dues like a FICA payment from a paycheck. Yet, young men coming in are VERY interested in charity. Their second question is usually "What do you guys do for the community?" *"Providing for our own retirement"* is not a good answer. Programs like the Masonic Angel Fund are perfect for this. It costs hardly anything to start and support, it helps local schools and children right in the Lodge's neighborhood, it takes no paperwork, and you can raise enough money to make a difference just sitting around the dining hall table. Twenty guys toss $10 on the table and it's funded for two months.

But the purpose of a Lodge is to teach a good man to be a better one, not to put a bumper sticker on his car that proclaims how much his club gives to help people every year. The purpose of Freemasonry is to teach charity and relief to its votaries, and then let them go forth to render such service to mankind through his own volition. This is not to criticize the wonderful works of the appendant bodies, but to encourage us to stop "selling" Freemasonry by stressing its charities to the exclusion of all else. Self-aggrandizing is ugly no matter how noble the intent may be.

The figure that Masons donate $2 million a day to charity is ten years out of date, and intellectually dishonest, since three quarters of that figure are from the Shrine alone. We need to stop dishonestly promoting ourselves on the coattails of the Shrine's philanthropy.

Masters need to stress to their members that they need to look *inward.* Plow snow-covered sidewalks for the Lodge widows. Fund a playground for the local park. Take up a collection for the neighbor whose house burned down. Wrap up the leftovers from a degree dinner and take them to an older shut-in member or widow. Or just pay a brother's dues for him when he's down on his luck. Charity does not just mean money. Our personal time is much harder to give, and therefore, more precious.

7. The Decline of Fellowship
"Do we pay enough attention to the Festive Board?"

"It was expedient to abolish the old custom of studying Geometry in the Lodge, and some younger Brethren made it appear that a good knife and fork, in the hands of a dexterous Brother, over proper Materials (food), would give great satisfaction and add more to the conviviality of the Lodge than the best Scale and Compasses in Europe."
-- Lawrence Dermott in "Ahiman Rezon"

In 1717, one of the reasons given for forming the Mother Grand Lodge in London was to hold the Annual Feast. Not a dinner, but a feast. The Festive Board is an event of celebration, a special occasion for brethren to meet, gather over good food in pleasant surroundings. The ceremonial toasts that were developed by our forefathers were meant to be an outpouring of emotion and brotherhood, not poorly read in a stilted table lodge ceremony.

The time is now to bring the Festive Board back to our fraternity. Hold it at a restaurant in a private room away from the lodge. Invite members from other lodges, and make it a true celebration of brotherhood and conviviality. Have an ENTERTAINING guest speaker on a Masonic or other subject. Unlike a table lodge, there is no ritual, other than perhaps celebrating the ceremonial toasts.

Then, there is the alcohol question, the dreaded third rail of Freemasonry. The alcohol ban should be lifted for both festive boards and for the renting of our facilities by outside groups. It is a parochial, antiquated law, enacted in the 1800's as part of a national temperance movement, and is completely anachronistic in light of our tavern-hall origins.

We talk about what we as Masons stand for, the upright character of the men in our rolls and the standards we demand of those who would wish to join us, then we fret over how our brethren would abuse the use of alcohol over dinner. It denies traditions that are even written into our rituals! The Junior Warden's job is to see that the Craft does not *"convert the purposes of refreshment into intemperance or excess."* We teach Temperance, not Abstinence. It is in our ritual, yet we don't even understand.

Arizona, California, Michigan, New Jersey, Florida, the District of Columbia, New Mexico, Iowa and Texas all allow liquor in their Lodge buildings during ceremonies or for room rentals, under varying degrees of circumstances and regulations. Most recently, the Grand Lodge of Oregon repealed its prohibition rules at its 2004 Annual Meeting. Outside of the United States, lodge feasts are, as a rule, accompanied by the sharing of wine. The New Connaught Rooms in London is a massive catering facility owned and operated by the United Grand Lodge of England. It is where most Lodges go for dinner and drinking after their meetings. The Grande Loge de France and the Grande Loge Nationale Française, both in Paris have very large dining and bar facilities in their buildings. They are all set up with private rooms as well, in case a lodge wishes to have a tyled Table Lodge. Predictably, our French brethren have very well-stocked wine cellars.

H. L. Haywood wrote in "More About Masonry,"

> *"In the Eighteenth Century Lodges the Feast bulked so large in the lodge that in many of them the members were seated at the table when the lodges were opened and remained at it throughout the Communication, even when the degrees were conferred. The result was that Masonic fellowship was good fellowship in it, as in a warm and fruitful soil, acquaintanceship, friendship, and affection could flourish - there was no grim and silent sitting on a bench, staring across at a wall. Out of this festal spirit flowered the love which Masons had for their lodge. They brought gifts to it, and only by reading of old inventories can any present day Mason measure the extent of that love; there were gifts of chairs, tables, altars, pedestals, tapestries, draperies, silver, candle-sticks, oil paintings, libraries, Bibles, mementos, curios, regalia's and portraits. The lodge was a home, warm, comfortable, luxurious, full of memories, and tokens, and affection, and even if a member died his, presence was never wholly absent; to such a lodge no member went*

grudgingly, nor had to be coaxed, nor was moved by that ghastly, cold thing called a sense of duty, but went as if drawn by a magnet, and counted the days until he could go.

"What business has any lodge to be nothing but a machine for grinding out the work: It was not called into existence in order to have the minutes read: Even a mystic tie will snap under the strain of cheerlessness, repetition, monotony, dullness. A lodge needs a fire lighted in it, and the only way to have that warmth is to restore the lodge Feast, because when it is restored, good fellowship and brotherly love will follow, and where good fellowship is, members will fill up an empty room not only with themselves but also with their gifts."

Somehow, American Masons decided that a Lodge should be a reverential place of piety, a temple to stern seriousness, bereft of anything but stated meetings and degrees, and if any fun was to be had, it should be over at the Shrine.

Our rules imply that a man, freeborn and well recommended is too untrustworthy to toast to his country, his fraternity, and his brethren with a glass of wine; that the use of such spirits was incompatible with Masonic ideals and traditions; and that engaging in the earliest tradition of our ancient brethren is now an apostasy within the walls of our Temples. Nothing could be farther from the truth.

So, what about the cost of insurance? What about the cost of liquor licenses? Won't our lodges be sued if a drunken member has an accident? Won't we make recovering alcoholic members uncomfortable? Just because the ban is lifted does not mean all or indeed ANY Lodge must allow alcohol onto their property. It merely would leave the decision in the hands of its members. Any Lodge so desiring it should be required by Grand Lodge regulations to have proper liability insurance coverage and any licensing required by state and local laws. The point is to allow the Lodge to decide how to best serve the desires of its members.

In their role as encouragers and promoters of the art, Grand Lodge could promote festive boards. Grand Officers could work with some of the more progressive lodges in their respective areas to create regional festive boards on a regular basis. Lodges will, hopefully, enjoy the experience and will need no further encouragement to continue the practice often. Think of the difference between a Feast of St. John with fifteen brothers assembled over a bowl of soup and a bologna sandwich, versus a county-wide gathering of Lodges, with a hundred or more men enjoying an excellent diner, singing and toasting.

8. Bread or Stone?

"What has become of that 'course of moral instruction, veiled in allegory and illustrated by symbols,' that Freemasonry is supposed to be?"

Promote greater education of our members. Provide better information to brand new members with study guides, books like Allen E. Roberts' *Symbols Of Freemasonry*, Chris Hodapp's *Freemasons For Dummies*, or S. Brent Morris' *Complete Idiot's Guide to Freemasonry*, and Kent Henderson's *Freemasonry for Wives*, along with specialized material from the Lodges themselves. By-Laws, officer's lists, membership lists, brochures, license plate forms, and blank petitions.

Do NOT remove the Q&A proficiency requirement, because it is required in other jurisdictions around the world as a test for entry, and because it gives new members a taste of learning ritual. Our standards must be higher, not lower.

Return the rights of the Entered Apprentice to him. Lodges should have the option to allow EAs in their meetings, if they so choose. This is the common practice all over the world, except in the United States. We tell a new EA that he "there stands a just and upright Mason," then slam the Lodge door in his face. Business meetings should be held on the EA degree. Doing so removes the velocity panic that encourages Lodges to move a man through the three degrees as fast as possible, without the new man comprehending the lessons of the work.

EAs and FCs in business meetings could not vote on motions, but could be allowed to sit on committees and participate immediately in the Lodge. They would be given greater opportunity to meet and get to know their fellow brethren. Opening on the EA also forces all officers to attend meetings and know their parts. If topics arise concerning the "secrets" of Master Masons, the EAs and FCs are simply escorted from the lodge room until the discussion is ended. Again, this is common practice in Masonry virtually everywhere but in the US.

In addition to reducing the "velocity panic" of conferring degrees as quickly as possible, we must also try to reduce the ferocious race to the Oriental Chair. It seems like as soon as a dedicated man is elected into the Lodge, there is a rush to jab him into an officer's chair with a Steward's rod. The advancing officer's line has institutionalized the custom of pushing a man as fast as possible through the chairs, into the East, and finally slamming him onto the sidelines as a Past Master. The resulting implication is that, once a man has served as Master of his Lodge, it's time to move on to something else, i.e. the Rites or the Shrine. It also encourages men who do not take an officer's chair to turn away from the Lodge because they are not part of the "inner circle" of the men running it.

A Lodge is about fellowship, participation, encouraging each man to do his best and to reach a little higher to accomplish things he might not have considered before— making him better. New and old members need to understand that each Mason is a link in the chain of the Lodge. Officers are needed, true, but so are mentors, cooks, accountants, janitors, ritualists, painters, and anyone else willing to donate his time and efforts towards improving his lodge and his fellow man. One need not be an officer to visit a widow or repair a candidate's garment or teach another member his catechism.

9. Bring the Line up to the Standard

"Hasn't the so-called 'Century of the Common Man' contributed to making our Fraternity a little too common?"

We did a great disservice to ourselves by expunging the word Temple from our buildings, as a reaction to clucking from the profane world. It's not a clubhouse, it's a temple of learning, a temple of ideas, a temple of friendship. It is where we go to celebrate our Brotherhood. Masonic Lodges are children of the Enlightenment, and it is time to start treating them that way again. Benjamin Franklin, Voltaire, Mozart all joined a Masonic Lodge to be with gentlemen who would debate the great questions of the day. We do not even understand who we are, or from where we've come. Masonry as philosophy needs to make a comeback.

Each lodge should adopt *some* kind of a dress code. If a man can't be bothered to wash his face and put on a clean pair of pants before walking through the door of a Masonic Temple he doesn't need to be there. If you don't care whether a man looks uncaring and unkempt when he walks through the door of your temple, YOU don't need to be there. We need to grow up and discover the joys of gentlemanly behavior. Not northern snooty phony gentlemanliness, but a genuine southern genteel gentlemanliness. If we cannot bother to put on a coat and tie at least when initiating, passing and raising a candidate, just how important an event will it strike that new man?

Where is our concentration on gentlemanliness? Why do we allow rude, coarse behavior among Masons? A recent Internet forum seriously discussed whether it was appropriate to turn away a brother who showed up at a funeral home to perform the solemn Masonic funeral service in jeans and a golf shirt! This is madness to even discuss, and pathetic that such disrespect to the deceased brother and his family would be so condoned by thinking Freemasons. "Hey! At least he showed up," is no excuse for crass disrespect of a solemn service.

It has been argued that society is less formal, more casual now, and that it is "the internal, not the external qualifications of a man that Masonry regards." True enough. But is it not also true that we say that we are making good men better ones? Is it not our job to polish our rough ashlar into a perfect one? Is it not true that we are expected to conduct ourselves as the BEST men in society, instead of aping the behavior of the common herd? If the world around us is rude and common, is it not our stated purpose to improve that world by improving men?

In Europe, Freemasonry is taken seriously because Freemasons take themselves seriously. European society takes the solemn "secret society" accusations to be plausible, because European Freemasons really do believe their fraternity is solemn, noble, exclusive, dignified and special. In America we are invisible and ignored. Perhaps it is because we no longer regard our fraternity with the respect and dignity the rest of society once did.

This does NOT mean that as a Temple, a lodge should be a stern, joyless place of dour ritualists. A lodge is, first and foremost, a place of Brotherhood, of friendships and close personal bonds. If it is nothing more than a degree mill to be opened, closed and fled, it is a failure. Again, our brethren outside of the U.S. never drove the fun out of their lodges, and as a result never saw the need to create Grottos and Shrines. The degrees of Masonry should be solemn. The business meeting should be brief. The Feast should be the centerpiece.

10. Let's Try Freemasonry
"Are there not too many well-meaning brethren who are working overtime to make Freemasonry something other than Freemasonry?"

A noted Grand Master often remarked, *"all Masonry is local."* The sooner Lodges come to this conclusion, the better. Grand Lodge will not solve the decline in membership in our Lodges. Visionary leadership, continuity of planning, and most important, the enthusiasm born of a small group of men who enjoy each other's company several nights a month will do more to save a Lodge than any Grand Scheme from Grand Lodge.

But one problem that DOES need to be addressed at every level of Freemasonry is one of visibility. Consider this quote from the Farmer's Almanac of 1823:

> *"A real Freemason is distinguished from the rest of Mankind by the uniform unrestricted rectitude of his conduct. Other men are honest in fear of punishment which the law might inflict; they are religious in expectation of being rewarded, or in dread of the devil in the next world. A Freemason would be just if there were no laws, human or divine except those written in his heart by the finger of his Creator. In every climate, under every system of religion, he is the same. He kneels before the Universal Throne of God in gratitude for the blessing he has received and humble solicitation for his future protection. He venerates the good men of all religions. He gives no offense, because he does not choose to be offended. He contracts no debts which he is certain he cannot discharge, because he is honest upon principle."*

In an age when pamphlets, broadsides and booklets like the Farmer's Almanac were what passed for mass media, the vast majority of Americans knew who Freemasons were and what they stood for. Consider the difference today. USAToday and ABC News aren't exactly singing our praises these days. Or even mentioning us, except to note the closing of another aging lodge.

Dwight Smith decried the promotion of the Craft as crass commercialism, that if we only "practiced Freemasonry" all would be put right again. But in the intervening four decades years since Smith wrote, two generations of men have been born who have no idea what Freemasonry is. They have no preconceived notions, because they've never heard of it. Men in their forties have heard the term, but don't know what it is. Men in their twenties and thirties have more than likely only heard of the Freemasons as mysterious villains in comic book fantasies and movies like *From Hell* and *The League of Extraordinary Gentlemen.* Thousands drive past magnificent temples, Scottish Rite and Shrine auditoriums every day without knowing what they are or that they have anything to do with Freemasons. Our Lodge buildings are nearly abandoned buildings, rarely with cars in the lot or any sign of activity.

The Scottish Rite and the Shrine have chosen to concentrate their efforts on promoting their charities as a way to garner publicity, and hopefully, interest. But as we have discussed, Freemasonry is not charity, and self-congratulatory back patting in public can backfire and take on the trappings of crass boasting.

So, what then are we to do to get into the eyes, ears and heads of modern young men who have no knowledge of us?

Advertising is a tricky thing. Recent billboards sponsored by the Grand Lodge of Indiana, for example, simply showed Masonic symbols and called attention to the Indiana Family of Masons. But it presupposed that the population knows who or what Masons are. We have a more daunting task now than we had in 1965. There is a vast population that does not know what the square and compasses mean, what a Freemason is and what we believe.

The Internet is the fastest growing method by which new members contact our Lodges. Every single lodge should have an up to date website. Visitors to Grand Lodge websites should easily be able to find a local Lodge by county and city, and be able to follow a link to communicate with that Lodge. And every lodge needs someone who will answer.

The Internet is also making the Masonic world smaller on a daily basis. Masons from around the world can now converse instantly. Questions of recognition and regularity must be more thoughtfully weighed and decided upon, and multiple Grand Lodges within the same geographical jurisdictions will be common in the future. The situation already exists in the U.S. with Prince Hall recognition. U.S. Grand Lodges that do not recognize their Prince Hall counterparts can no longer hide institutionalized racism behind the façade of regularity or the discredited doctrine of territorial exclusivity. The same should be true in foreign jurisdictions where multiple, regular Grand Lodges stubbornly shun each other. Ignoring these issues will only be detrimental to the future of Freemasonry. Grand Lodges are sovereign bodies, and the political pressure brought to bear against the Grand Lodge of Minnesota by New York and other grand lodges over its attempts to recognize the regular Grande Loge de France in 2002 was unconscionable.

Young professional men who seek out this fraternity do not find institutional segregation in their jobs, their lunch counters, their housing, their government, their

27

media or anywhere else in their daily lives. To discover it in Freemasonry, an institution that purports to encourage universal brotherhood, is nothing short of repulsive. Grand Lodges that continue to engage in racism – regardless of how they justify it – and allow their members to openly espouse racism with impunity, do so at the risk of their own survival. The Civil Rights Act was passed four decades ago. We should at least bring ourselves forward into the 1960s. By failing to do so, increasing numbers of young men will regard us as completely irrelevant in a modern society. And rightly so.

The Internet is spreading knowledge of foreign Masonic practices. Cookie-cutter demands that each Lodge must look, feel and act alike are stifling and ignore human behavior. In England and elsewhere it is common for many rituals to be worked within a given jurisdiction under the same Grand Lodge. It should not be unlawful to for a Lodge to work Emulation, Scottish Rite or other alternative but regular rituals for the three degrees. Greater variety means greater knowledge and deeper understanding of our heritage. We must not simply stick our heads in the Masonic sands and pretend other rituals do not exist.

Every single Lodge should have posted on its door times of meetings for every group that gathers in that building, along with contact information, and the website address. How can a good man ask to join if he can't find your Lodge, or can't find someone to answer his questions?

Lodges in smaller communities have a better opportunity to get their events publicized in local papers or on radio stations. The media doesn't know who or what we are either. Invite the local news media to tour our buildings, to interview our leaders or our youngest, most eager members. The world thinks we are dead and dying, so we need to beat on the coffin lid until they hear us.

At one time, our buildings were places both physically and philosophically in the center of our communities, and they should be again. They *could* be open from morning till night, occupied six days a week. A place where retirees could come and have coffee and donuts and play cards every day, maybe catch up on their e-mail or make use of the library or a book exchange. Every evening there might be cards or pool or darts or a Play Station tournament, a dinner and a meeting of one of the many Lodges or bodies that meet there. Maybe a movie going on the big screen TV. Maybe a practice night for a Degree Club of members from lots of lodges who meet to work and travel the county putting on the degrees. Maybe once a month a pitch-in barbecue or even a campfire.

And finally, remember that each Mason is a walking advertisement—good or bad—for the Fraternity. A Square and Compass on our hats, jackets, shirts, license plates and rings can start a conversation, but our behavior and actions speak louder than any billboard, bumper sticker or radio ad.

Freemasonry is an ideal, a design. Human nature can lead to the ignoring of our teachings, but Nature is what we are put in this world to rise above. We must continually encourage ourselves and our brethren to "try Freemasonry." Masters need to put a stop to the bickering that can go on in a meeting, in a friendly manner. Officers at the Lodge and Grand Lodge level need to go out of the room and count to ten before considering engaging in un-Masonic arguments, political maneuvering or use of power and position to exact revenge. Brother means "brother," and we must be slow to explode and quick to forgive. Charity among brethren should mean far more than money.

A man walking away from his Lodge or the fraternity is a terrible loss, but too many do just that after seeing that what we practice is a far cry from what we preach. We must continually remind ourselves that we strive to have no contention within our Temples, and endeavor to emulate those who can best work or best agree.

PART FOUR

WHITHER ARE WE TRAVELING?

As long as most of us have been Freemasons, we have heard about dwindling numbers, lack of participation, shoddy degree work, and the rest of the litany of ills that confront us. Freemasons have spent nearly half a century identifying the problems. We KNOW the problems.

The concepts that have been discussed are all possible steps to solutions. Not one, enormous golden magic wand that will pack our Lodge rooms to the rafters with eager minds—but a whole range of ideas that, taken as a whole, will change behavior, change attitudes, and change the direction we are headed. They are small and large, at both the Grand Lodge and local level.

We have charted a path to return us to the place from whence we came. We advocate not turning back the clock, but rather, a return to the precepts of what made Freemasonry grow and prosper in its infancy, so that it might do so again. We do not advocate the dismantling of all that is new, only that which has been destructive and divisive.

North American Freemasonry is in decline, both numerically and philosophically. Mathematically, numbers of Masons dwindle as we see the passing of Brothers from the "membership bubble" of the 1940's through the 1960's. The decades following their initiation brought fewer and fewer new men into the fraternity, and what was once universally known as the greatest, most noble men's organization in the world has all but disappeared from the public consciousness.

Philosophically, the decline is much older. At its historic core, Freemasonry was an initiatic experience, an exclusive gathering of men who valued learning, strove for excellence in intellectual, social and charitable pursuits, strenuously participated in shaping their governments and societies, all while joyously celebrating the regular gathering and comradeship of their regular meetings. All of this was done on the level, among men of all faiths and economic strata. It was not exclusive in its makeup, but once made a Mason, a member was to strive for excellence in every intellectual, social and charitable detail. It was expensive and hard to join, demanding in its rules of conduct, and expected its members to always improve themselves and each other—

not unlike the Craft Guilds the fraternity fashioned itself after.

These original precepts have become forgotten and, over the last century, North American Freemasonry has lost its way. Artificially swollen in ranks by the massive influx of post-WWII members, Grand Lodges now see shrinking numbers merely as a failure of recruiting techniques. Successive Grand Masters hold themselves responsible for finding new ways to restore numerical growth, only to erode the foundations of the fraternity that made it so unique in the first place. Such schemes are not to blame for our plight, but they are shortsighted in their neglect of the long-term condition of Masonry.

We will survive. But survive as what?

The real hope for our survival lies at the doorstep of the local Lodge, not the halls of Grand Lodge. No one idea, plan or program will be the magic bullet that saves us from a slow death. The time has come to devolve power into the hands of the local Lodges, so they may better serve the needs of their local members. Instead of central planning, we have hundreds of laboratories to experiment in, within the confines of the Ancient Landmarks. Instead of demanding "cookie-cutter," one-size-fits-all Lodges, each Lodge should have its own distinct personality.

Almost a century ago, on June 13, 1912, the Reverend Joseph Fort Newton, a famous Freemason and Christian Minister, addressed the Grand Lodge of Iowa, brilliantly illuminating why the leaders of the Craft needed to take care with what they did to this fraternity, and emphasizing to us today why we must seize the moment before it passes and we have lost it for good:

> *"Those sturdy men who set up the altar of Masonry on the frontier of this commonwealth were prophetic souls. They were men of faith who builded better than they knew, as men of faith always do. They believed in the future, in the growth of large things from small beginnings and in the principles of Masonry as the true foundation of society and the fortress of a free state. They knew that the Masonic lodge is a silent partner of the home, the church, and the school house, toiling on behalf of law and order, without which neither industry nor art can flourish, and that its benign influence would help us to build a commonwealth in strength, wisdom, and beauty. Therefore they erected their altar and kindled its flame; and having wrought in faithfulness, they died in faith, obeying the injunction of that master poet who said: 'Keep the young generations in hail, bequeath to them no tumbled house!'"*

-- Joseph Fort Newton
The Men's House: Masonic Papers and Addresses
(Masonic Service Association, 1923)

There is another way than the one we have been following for decades. We owe an irreparable debt to all those men who have come before us, those guardians of the Temple who kept the lamp lit and passed this fraternity into our care. What we do—or fail to do—now will either be the slow end or a new beginning for the coming generations of Freemasons, who, as we have looked to the brethren who preceded us, will look to *us* for the sort of leadership that made this a legendary brotherhood. The answer to that challenge is in our hands, *and in our hands alone*

"Bequeath to them no tumbled house!"

Afterward

An outline for discussion and legislation

1. EAs and FCs should be allowed into our business meetings. They have been since the fraternity began, in every corner of the globe except in the US after the 1840's. It is US Masonry that created an innovation in the body of Freemasonry. It's time we stopped it.

2. Provide better leadership at the Grand Lodge level by allowing nominations from the floor. The current system of appointment to the line by the sitting Grand Master is flawed, irresponsible and subject to potential abuse, however well-liked and well-meaning the Grand Master may be.

3. Provide better leadership at the Lodge level by ending the reliance on the progressive officer's line. If a man is not qualified, he should not make the jump from SD to JW, nor should he ascend to the East just because he has put in his time. Contrary to conventional wisdom, one unqualified Master can indeed wreck a Lodge in a year.

4. Educate our members and our officers in our history, in our customs and in our duties. That means Masonic education, leadership training, and the simple skills of being gentlemen. Develop a course of instruction for Wardens based on the ritual and leadership skills they will need, and make its completion a requirement for election as Master.

5. Raise the standards of our conduct and our work, not lower them. That means proficiency and attendance requirements, dress codes, and real investigations of new members. That does NOT mean that we should be excluding men because of social standing, profession or religion. It DOES mean that once a man is a Mason, he is to strive to be the best.

6. Eliminate the power of the Grand Master to suspend without an immediate trial. When the GM suspends a member, a Trial Commission should be convened within a reasonable period of time, and must be made up of Past Masters, NOT Past Grand Masters or Grand Line officers.

7. Repeal the prohibition of alcohol for renters of Lodge buildings and at Masonic banquets. We teach Temperance, not Abstinence. It is long past time that we treat each other as adults, as our brethren everywhere outside of the United States do.

8. Raise our dues and petition fees to a level reasonable enough to ensure financial stability, and high enough to encourage participation and value. Any Lodge charging less than $100 a year (in 2006) is cheating itself and cheapening the fraternity.

9. Adopt long-range plans for financial stability in the face of dwindling numbers, at both the Grand Lodge and local Lodge level. Successive leaders need to sign on to such plans and be involved in their design at an early stage, not just in "their year." Reinventing the wheel every year is destructive, irresponsible and foolish.

10. End our preoccupation with saving the appendant bodies. New Masons should wait one year after being raised before joining an appendant body. The Lodge is not responsible for the troubles of other groups that compete for our members' reduced free time and discretionary cash. The other members of the Masonic family have a lifetime to seek a man's participation. Let's make him a Freemason first.

11. Encourage local Lodges to have their own personality, style and customs. Cookie-cutter demands that each Lodge must look, feel and act alike are stifling and ignore human behavior. In England and elsewhere it is common for many rituals to be worked within a given jurisdiction under the same Grand Lodge. It should not be unlawful to for a Lodge to work Emulation, Scottish Rite or other alternative but regular rituals for the three degrees. Greater variety means greater knowledge and deeper understanding of our heritage. We must not simply stick our heads in the Masonic sands and pretend other rituals do not exist.

12. Slow down, not speed up our degree process. One-day classes will quickly die by running out of candidates who want to participate in such mass raisings. They are already shrinking in popularity and becoming less successful in every year and in every jurisdiction that tries them. New Masons want to learn and understand before moving on.

13. The internet is making the Masonic world smaller on a daily basis. Masons from around the world can converse instantly. Questions of recognition and regularity must be more thoughtfully weighed and decided upon, and multiple Grand Lodges within the same jurisdictions will be common in the future. That situation already exits in the US with Prince Hall recognition. The same should be true in foreign jurisdictions where multiple, regular Grand Lodges stubbornly shun each other. Ignoring these issues will only be detrimental to the future of Freemasonry.

Who are the Knights of the North?

There is no one author of this work. The ideas herein stemmed from Internet discussions among many friends and brothers between 2003 and 2006. They are Master Masons, Past Masters, and Past Grand Masters—some new to the fraternity, some with decades of service, and many somewhere in between. Original members included Timothy Bonney, Nathan Brindle, Christopher Hodapp, Jeffrey Naylor, Eric Schmitz and many others. Since the original preparation of this paper, the Knights of the North have grown in number. They continue to propose positive, realistic, and concrete recommendations for the future of the fraternity.

Einstein told us, *"The definition of insanity is doing the same thing over and over again and expecting a different result."* It is our desire to break that cycle that has atrophied Freemasonry into its current state. It is NOT our desire to engage in a battle of personalities, but change must come from within our organization before it is thrust upon us by time, society, and circumstances. It is our desire to encourage our present leaders—and especially those who will lead us a decade from now—to embrace these proposals and act upon them.

– Christopher L. Hodapp, Editor